For:

Holiday
COOKIES
∾ *and* ∾
CHOCOLATE
with Music

Compiled by Evelyn L. Beilenson

Illustrations by James Henry

PETER PAUPER PRESS, INC.
WHITE PLAINS, NEW YORK

To Ethel Mills, for her help in testing many of the recipes herein, and for her friendship.

Copyright © 1993, 1996
Peter Pauper Press, Inc.
202 Mamaroneck Avenue
White Plains, NY 10601
All rights reserved
ISBN 0-88088-861-X
Printed in Singapore
7 6 5 4 3 2 1

How to Work with Chocolate and recipes entitled *Chocolate-Coated Strawberries, Chocolate Swirl Lace Cookies, Double Chip Cookies, Chocolate Sauce,* and *Chocolate Pecan Pumpkin Muffins* copyright © 1986 by Peter G. Rose and used with her permission.

Interior book design by Deborah Michel
Border and chapter opening illustrations by Grace DeVito
Title page illustration by Lori Nelson Field

CONTENTS

CHOCOLATE

How to Work with Chocolate

In baking, chocolate may be replaced by cocoa, using the following rule of thumb: 3 level tablespoons of cocoa + 1 level tablespoon shortening = 1 square of baking chocolate.

☞ In candy-making, remember that chocolate is highly temperamental, and easily influenced by any change in temperature or humidity. The ideal working environment is about 65° F. with 50% or less humidity.

☞ To melt chocolate, use a double boiler but do not let the water in the bottom come to a boil. Any water drops or steam that get into the chocolate will make it grainy. *Chocolate should be melted slowly, at a temperature for white chocolate no higher than 115° and for dark chocolate no higher than 120°.* Chop chocolate into small pieces, place 1/3 in the top of the double boiler, stir, and let melt. Gradually add more chopped chocolate, melt, stir, and continue to add more until all is melted.

☞ As an alternative, you can melt chocolate on a warming tray set on high (as do some professional chocolatiers).

☞ Tempering, a method which requires the raising and lowering of the temperature of melted chocolate, insures that it sets rapidly and has the warm gloss which looks so appetizing in professionally coated bonbons and other candies. Discussions of how to temper chocolate can be found in books on chocolate candy-making. None of the recipes in this book requires tempering.

☞ Finally, you can place chocolate in a small glass or ceramic dish in the microwave for 1-1/2 minutes on high. Then remove and stir to finish melting.

☞ Although these explanations may be a bit daunting, the recipes that follow are easy to do and well worth the effort. Even if things go wrong, there will never be any waste, because, as Sandra Boynton states in *Chocolate, the Consuming Passion* (Workman Publishing, New York, 1982): *Unsuccessful fudge makes an excellent ice cream topping; unsuccessful brownies make an unusual and delicious pudding; an unsuccessful chocolate soufflé makes an attractive beret.*

NOTE: In testing, unsalted butter and large eggs were used. All baking requires a preheated oven.

CHOCOLATE TRUFFLES

3/4 cup heavy cream

8 ounces semisweet or dark sweet chocolate, coarsely chopped

2 tablespoons dark rum, brandy, Amaretto, or other liqueur (optional)

Choice of coatings:
Unsweetened cocoa
Chocolate sprinkles
Finely chopped almonds, pecans, or walnuts

Place cream in medium size heavy saucepan. Cook over moderate heat just until bubbles begin to form around edges of cream. Add chocolate and cook, stirring, about 2 minutes. Remove from heat and continue stirring until chocolate is completely melted. Cool to room temperature and stir in liqueur. Spoon into bowl, cover loosely with waxed paper, and place in refrigerator at least 2 hours or until thickened, stirring occasionally.

Line cookie sheet with waxed paper. Dust hands

lightly with confectioners sugar or cocoa. Form chocolate mixture into 1-inch balls and place balls on lined cookie sheet. Place cookie sheet, uncovered, in refrigerator at least ten minutes or until truffles are firm.

Line second cookie sheet with waxed paper and set aside. One coating may be used for all truffles or a variety of coatings may be used. Place each coating on separate piece of waxed paper and roll truffles gently in coating. Place coated truffles on freshly lined cookie sheet and return to refrigerator, uncovered, until firm.

When truffles are firm, place in miniature paper cups, if desired, and place between layers of waxed paper in tightly covered container. Store in refrigerator. About 2 dozen truffles.

HINTS AND TIPS:

Unwanted moisture can cause disaster when working with chocolate. Use dry utensils, *never* cover a pan in which chocolate is being melted, and don't try to make truffles on a rainy or humid day. Even as little as one drop of water can cause chocolate to stiffen.

Chocolate should be melted over low or moderate heat. High heat will cause chocolate to burn.

Traditionally, unsweetened cocoa is used to coat truffles. If you find the flavor of unsweetened cocoa too bitter, be untraditional and use sweetened cocoa instead.

The quality and flavor of a truffle are directly related to the quality of chocolate used. Buy the very best quality chocolate you can afford.

BARBARA BLOCH

Melt-in-Your-Mouth Truffles

1 cup minus 1 tablespoon heavy cream
4 tablespoons butter
1 14-ounce package chocolate chips
4 tablespoons finely chopped walnuts
1 teaspoon grated orange zest (use orange part of skin only)
3/4 ounce Frangelico
3/4 ounce Cointreau
1/2 cup cocoa

Bring cream and butter to a boil in double boiler. Add chocolate and stir until chocolate has dissolved. Makes 2-1/3 cups ganache (truffle mixture). Divide between two bowls. Cool slightly. Add walnuts to one batch and orange zest to the other. Cool completely. Slowly add Frangelico to first batch while beating mixture with an electric handmixer. Do not overbeat. Repeat process with second batch, using Cointreau. Freeze both batches. To shape truffles: Remove ganache from freezer. Shape semi-thawed ganache into 1-inch balls, using a melon-ball cutter. Chill. Working with a few at a time, put each truffle into a dish with cocoa and roll to coat. Keep truffles refrigerated. About 48 truffles.

JANE WONG

CHOCOLATE-COATED STRAWBERRIES

1 pint strawberries
1 5-oz. bar milk (sweet) chocolate

Carefully wash strawberries. (They usually are quite gritty and might also have been sprayed with pesticides.) Leave green tops on. Pat dry thoroughly with paper towels. Melt chocolate in a small dish on a warming tray. Spear each fruit on a 7-inch bamboo skewer, but do not push it all the way through. Dip each strawberry in melted chocolate. With a small rubber spatula, spread an even, neat-looking coating covering about three-quarters of each berry. Push other end of each skewer into an orange, grapefruit, or green cabbage (depending on how many strawberries you are dipping). Refrigerate at least an hour until strawberries are ice-cold and coating is hard. Serve straight from the refrigerator.

CHOCOLATE ALMOND CRUNCHIES

1/2 cup butter, softened
1 tablespoon brown sugar
2 tablespoons white sugar
1 teaspoon vanilla
1/2 cup toasted almonds, chopped
1/2 cup miniature chocolate chips
1 cup sifted flour

Combine all ingredients and mix thoroughly. Shape into 1-inch balls. Bake at 350° for 15 minutes. Check after 10 minutes (the bottoms tend to burn). Remove from oven and roll in confectioners sugar while still warm. 36 cookies.

HARRIET B. RISLEY

CHOCOLATE SWIRL LACE COOKIES

8 tablespoons butter, softened
2/3 cup sugar
1 cup flour
1/2 teaspoon vanilla
1 tablespoon cocoa

Cream butter with sugar and add flour. Stir to combine thoroughly. Divide dough in half. To one half add the vanilla, to the other the cocoa. Roll out balls of dough into equal size rectangles. Place chocolate dough rectangle on top and roll together lengthwise, jelly-roll fashion. Refrigerate for 30 minutes. Cut dough into 1/4-inch thick slices. Place slices 2 inches apart on an ungreased baking sheet. Bake at 350° for 12 minutes. Remove promptly. 36 cookies.

CHOCOLATE ROLL

5 large eggs, separated
2/3 cup sugar
6 oz. semi-sweet chocolate
3 tablespoons strong coffee
Cocoa
1-1/4 cups heavy cream, whipped

Butter a 12 x 8-inch baking sheet. Line it with waxed paper and butter paper. Beat egg yolks and sugar with a rotary beater or electric mixer until thick and pale in color. Combine chocolate and coffee and place over low heat. Stir until chocolate melts. Let mixture cool slightly, then stir it into egg yolks. Beat egg whites until stiff and fold them in. Spread mixture evenly on prepared baking sheet and bake 15 minutes at 350°, or until a knife inserted in the middle comes out clean. Do not overbake.

Remove pan from oven and cover cake with a damp cloth. Let stand 30 minutes or until cool. Loosen cake from baking sheet and dust cake generously with cocoa. Turn cake out on waxed paper, cocoa side down, and carefully remove paper from bottom of cake. Spread cake with whipped cream, sweetened and flavored to taste, and roll up like a jelly roll. For easy rolling, firmly grasp each corner of waxed paper on which cake was turned out and flip over about two inches of the edge on top of cake. Continue to roll by further lifting waxed paper. The last roll should deposit the log on a long platter. Cover top with whipped cream. Garnish with chocolate shavings. 8 servings.

DOUBLE CHIP COOKIES

1/2 cup butter, softened
1 cup sugar
2 eggs
1 teaspoon vanilla
2-1/4 cups flour
2 teaspoons baking powder
1/4 teaspoon salt
1/2 cup miniature chocolate chips
1/2 cup butterscotch chips cut in halves

Cream together butter and sugar. Add eggs and vanilla and combine thoroughly. Sift together dry ingredients and add to butter mixture. Stir in chips. Shape dough into 1-inch balls and place them on a greased baking sheet. Flatten balls with a floured glass. Bake at 375° for about 12 minutes. They will remain light on top. Remove and cool. Store in an airtight container. 36 cookies.

CHOCOLATE SAUCE

1 tablespoon butter
2 squares unsweetened chocolate
3/4 cup sugar
3/4 cup milk
1/4 teaspoon salt
1/2 teaspoon vanilla

Melt butter and chocolate; stir in sugar and milk alternately a little at a time. When all is combined, stir in salt and vanilla. This makes a glossy, thick sauce. Serve at room temperature.

HOT CHOCOLATE SOUFFLÉ

1/2 cup sugar, divided
1/3 cup unsweetened cocoa
1/4 cup flour
1/8 teaspoon salt
1 cup milk
1/2 teaspoon vanilla
4 eggs, separated

Combine 1/4 cup of the sugar, cocoa, flour, and salt in medium saucepan. Stir in milk. Cook over medium heat, stirring constantly, until mixture boils and is smooth and thickened. Stir in vanilla. Set aside. Prepare soufflé dish by buttering thoroughly and sprinkling with superfine sugar. Beat egg whites at high speed in large mixing bowl until foamy. Add remaining sugar, 2 tablespoons at a time, beating constantly until sugar is dissolved and whites are glossy and stiff enough that they will not slip when bowl is tilted. (To feel if sugar has dissolved, rub a bit of meringue between thumb and forefinger.) Thoroughly blend egg yolks into reserved sauce. Gently, but thoroughly, fold yolk mixture into whites. Pour carefully into 1-1/2 to 2-quart soufflé dish or casserole. Bake in preheated oven at 350° until soufflé is puffy and delicately browned, and soufflé shakes slightly when oven rack is gently moved back and forth (about 30 to 40 minutes). Serve immediately.

AMERICAN EGG BOARD

CHOCOLATE MOUSSE

5 eggs, separated
4 oz. semisweet chocolate chips
3 tablespoons sugar
1/2 pint heavy cream
2 tablespoons brandy

Beat egg yolks. Melt chocolate chips in top of double boiler. Remove chocolate from stove and add beaten egg yolks. Mix thoroughly. Add sugar to heavy cream in another bowl and beat until whipped. Add whipped cream to chocolate mixture. Beat egg whites until stiff and fold into chocolate mixture. Add brandy. Pour into serving bowl and refrigerate for at least 10 hours.

LA GOURMANDISE BROWNIES

1 cup lightly salted butter, softened
3 3-ounce bars bittersweet European chocolate, melted
*   and cooled*
6 eggs, at room temperature
1-3/4 cups sugar
1/4 teaspoon vanilla
2-1/2 cups all-purpose flour
Confectioners sugar

Use a wire whisk to prepare this entire recipe. Combine butter and melted chocolate. In a separate bowl combine thoroughly the eggs and sugar, but do not overbeat. Stir in vanilla. Add flour, then chocolate mixture, to sugar and eggs. Again, do not overmix. Pour batter into buttered 12 x 8-1/2-inch pan and bake at 300° for 25 to 30 minutes. Do not overbake; these brownies should be soft in the middle. Cool. Dust heavily with confectioners sugar. Refrigerate overnight. Cut into 1-inch squares.

CHOCOLATE PECAN PUMPKIN MUFFINS

2-1/2 cups sugar
1 cup salad oil
4 eggs
2 cups pumpkin, cooked and mashed, or canned
3 cups flour
1/2 teaspoon baking powder
1 teaspoon baking soda
1/2 teaspoon salt
1-1/2 teaspoons cinnamon
1 teaspoon freshly grated nutmeg
1 cup pecans, chopped
1 cup miniature chocolate chips

Combine sugar and oil; add eggs and beat until thoroughly incorporated. Stir in pumpkin. Sift together dry ingredients and add to sugar mixture. Add pecans and chocolate chips; stir to combine thoroughly. Fill muffin cups 3/4 full. Bake at 350° for 20 to 25 minutes, or until a toothpick inserted comes out clean. Serve warm or cold.

CHOCOLATE PECAN PIE

1-1/2 ounces unsweetened baking chocolate
3 tablespoons butter
3 eggs, lightly beaten
1 cup sugar
1/2 cup corn syrup
1 cup pecans, broken
1 unbaked pie shell

Melt chocolate and butter in double boiler. Cool slightly. Add beaten eggs to chocolate mixture. Then beat in sugar and corn syrup with whisk. Add pecans. Fill unbaked pie shell with mixture and bake for 10 minutes at 400°, then for 30 to 35 minutes at 350°. Serve either cold or hot. Delicious topped with whipped cream.

COOKIES

Greetings!

Mix your batter gaily,
Choose a colored bowl;
Make a cheerful clatter,
Whistle as you roll!

The cookies will be better,
The afternoon less long,
If you do your baking
To a tuneful song!

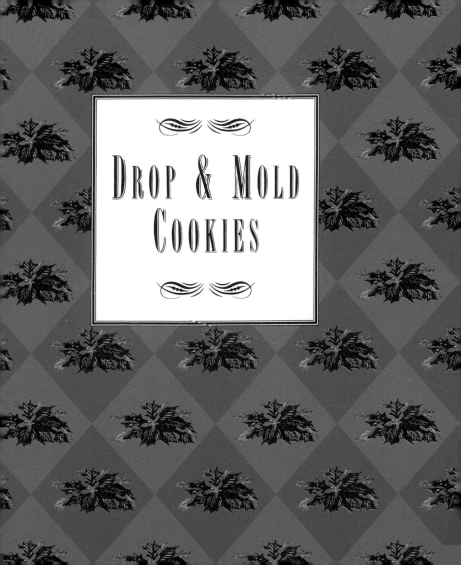

DROP & MOLD
COOKIES

SNOW DROPS

1 cup soft butter
1/2 cup confectioners sugar (sifted if lumpy)
1/4 teaspoon salt
3/4 cup finely chopped walnuts
2-1/4 cups flour
Confectioners sugar

Mix first 4 ingredients thoroughly. Work in flour with hands. Chill dough. Roll into balls about 1 inch in diameter. Bake at 350° on ungreased cookie sheets until set—not brown—for about 10-12 minutes. Let stand for an hour to dry. Then roll in confectioners sugar. 40 cookies.

CINNAMON NIBBLES

1-1/4 cups sifted flour
1 teaspoon baking powder
1/4 teaspoon salt
1/2 cup soft butter
1 cup sugar
1 beaten egg
1 teaspoon vanilla
1/2 cup finely chopped nuts
2 teaspoons cinnamon

Sift together flour, baking powder, salt. Mix, until creamy, butter, sugar, egg, and vanilla. Mix in flour mixture. Chill 1 hour. Shape level tablespoons of dough into balls; roll balls in combined nuts and cinnamon. Arrange on greased cookie sheet, 2 inches apart. Bake in 350° oven for 12 minutes. 30 cookies.

OLD-FASHIONED SOFT COOKIES

2 cups sifted flour
1/2 teaspoon baking soda
1/2 teaspoon salt
1/2 cup soft butter
1 cup sugar
1 egg yolk
1/2 cup buttermilk or sour milk
1/2 teaspoon vanilla
1 egg white

Sift together first 3 ingredients. Mix butter, sugar, and egg yolk until fluffy. Mix in flour mixture alternately with buttermilk; then mix in vanilla. Fold in egg white, beaten stiff. Drop by tablespoonfuls, 3 inches apart, onto greased cookie sheet. Flatten with spatula to 1/2 inch thickness. Bake until golden brown in 350° oven, about 15 minutes. 18 cookies.

OATMEAL HERMITS

1-1/2 cups sifted flour
2 teaspoons baking powder
1/2 teaspoon salt
1/2 teaspoon cinnamon
2 cups rolled oats
1 cup raisins
1/2 cup butter
1 cup sugar
2 eggs
1/2 cup milk

Sift together flour, baking powder, salt, and cinnamon; stir in oats and raisins. Cream butter; gradually beat in sugar, then eggs. Stir in flour and oats mixture alternately with milk. Drop from teaspoon on greased baking sheet and bake in 350° oven about 12 minutes. 36 cookies.

KRIS KRINGLES

1/2 cup butter
1/4 cup sugar
1 beaten egg yolk
1 tablespoon grated orange peel
1 teaspoon grated lemon peel
1 teaspoon lemon juice
1 cup flour
1/8 teaspoon salt
1 slightly beaten egg white
1/2 cup chopped walnuts
10 candied cherries

Cream butter and sugar; add egg yolk, orange and lemon peel, and lemon juice. Beat thoroughly. Stir in flour and salt. Chill until firm. Form balls about 1/2 inch in diameter. Dip in egg white and roll lightly in nuts. Place on greased cookie sheet; press 1/2 candied cherry in center of each. Bake in 325° oven about 20 minutes. 20 cookies.

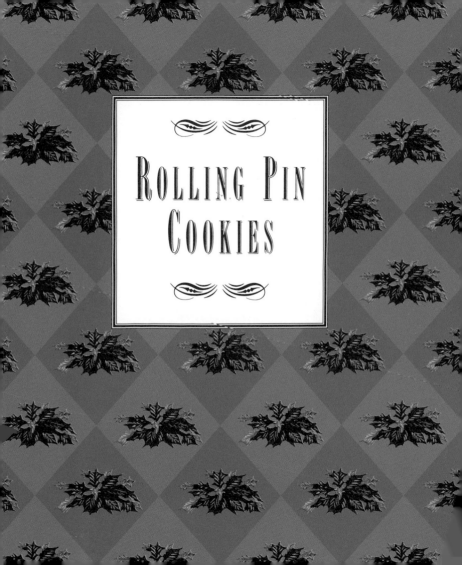

ROLLING PIN COOKIES

SUGAR COOKIES

1/2 cup soft butter
1/2 cup sugar
1 egg
1 tablespoon milk or cream
1/2 teaspoon vanilla
1/2 teaspoon lemon extract
1-1/2 cups flour
1/2 teaspoon baking soda
1/4 teaspoon salt
Colored sugar

Combine ingredients in above order. Chill dough. Roll out very thin, about 1/16-inch thick. Cut into fancy shapes with cookie cutters. Sprinkle with colored sugar and bake at 350° on greased cookie sheets until very lightly browned—about 5 to 6 minutes. Watch carefully to keep from over-browning. About 80 small cookies.

GINGERBREAD MEN

1-1/4 cups sifted flour
3/4 teaspoon baking soda
1/2 teaspoon ginger
1/2 cup molasses
1/4 cup soft butter
1 teaspoon grated orange rind
Raisins and candied fruits for decoration

Sift together first 3 ingredients. Bring molasses and shortening to boil in sauce pan; cool slightly. Add flour mixture and orange rind; mix well. Chill thoroughly. Roll dough to 1/8-inch thickness. Cut with man shaped cookie cutter. Decorate with small raisins and bits of candied fruits. Bake on greased cookie sheet, 1/2 inch apart, 8 to 10 minutes in 350° oven. 36 men.

GINGER COOKIES

1/2 cup shortening
1/2 cup sugar
1/2 cup light molasses
1/2 tablespoon vinegar
1 beaten egg
3 cups all-purpose flour
1/4 teaspoon salt
1/2 teaspoon baking soda
1/2 teaspoon cinnamon
1/2 teaspoon ginger

Bring shortening, sugar, molasses, and vinegar to boil.
Cool and add egg. Add sifted dry ingredients; mix well.
Shape into roll and chill. Cut into rounds 1/4-inch thick.
Bake on greased cookie sheet in 375° oven for 15
minutes. 30 cookies.

BROWN SUGAR COOKIES

4 eggs
1 pound brown sugar
1-1/2 cups flour
1-1/2 teaspoons baking powder
1 pinch salt
1/2 teaspoon vanilla
2 cups pecans
Juice of 1/2 lemon

Beat eggs and brown sugar together. Cook in double boiler about 20 minutes, until thick. Combine with remainder of ingredients. Roll dough out, cut in desired shapes, and bake in 350° oven about 20 minutes.

BARS
& SQUARES

APRICOT BARS

2/3 cup dried apricots
1/2 cup soft butter
1/4 cup sugar
1-1/3 cups sifted flour, divided
1/2 teaspoon baking powder
1/4 teaspoon salt
1 cup brown sugar
2 well-beaten eggs
1/2 teaspoon vanilla
1/2 cup chopped nuts
Confectioners sugar

Rinse apricots; cover with water; boil 10 minutes. Drain, cool, and chop. Mix, until crumbly, butter, sugar, and 1 cup flour. Pack into greased shallow, square pan. Bake in 350° oven about 8 minutes, or until lightly browned. Sift together remaining 1/3 cup flour, baking powder, and salt. Gradually beat brown sugar into eggs. Add flour mixture; mix well. Mix in vanilla, nuts, apricots. Spread over baked layer. Bake 40 minutes in 350° oven, or until done. Cool in pan; cut into bars; roll in confectioners sugar. 32 bars.

BROWNIES

2/3 cup sifted flour
1/2 teaspoon baking powder
3/4 teaspoon salt
1 cup sugar
1/2 cup soft butter
2 eggs
1 teaspoon vanilla
2 squares unsweetened chocolate, melted
1 cup chopped walnuts

Sift together first 3 ingredients. Gradually add sugar to butter, mixing until light. Add eggs and vanilla; mix until smooth. Blend in chocolate, then flour mixture and walnuts. Turn into greased pan. Bake in 350° oven 30 minutes. Cool in pan; cut into squares. 16 brownies.

SPECIAL GIFT COOKIES

BROWN LACE COOKIES

2 cups brown sugar
1/4 cup butter
2 eggs, well beaten
1 teaspoon vanilla
1 teaspoon baking powder
1/2 cup flour
1/2 pound pecans, cut coarse

Cream sugar and butter; add eggs and vanilla. Add baking powder to flour and mix with nuts, and combine the two mixtures. Chill until firm, 1 hour or more.

Drop by 1/2 teaspoonfuls 3 inches apart on buttered and floured cookie sheet. Bake at 350° until golden brown. Remove from pan when slightly cooled.

HUNGARIAN RUGELACH

1 cup soft sweet butter
1/2 pound soft cream cheese
1/4 teaspoon salt
2 cups sifted flour
1 cup chopped walnuts
1/2 cup sugar
1 tablespoon cinnamon

Mix butter, cheese, and salt until creamy. Mix in flour. Shape into 14 balls. Chill overnight. On lightly floured, cloth-covered board, roll each ball into 6-inch circle. Cut each into quarters. Mix nuts, sugar, cinnamon. Drop rounded teaspoonful of nut mixture on each quarter. Pinch edges of dough together, then form into crescents. Place on ungreased cookie sheet. Bake until light brown in a 325° oven for about 12 minutes. About 50 cookies.

VIENNESE CRESCENTS

1 cup soft butter
1/3 cup sugar
2/3 cup chopped almonds
1/4 teaspoon salt
2 cups flour
Confectioners sugar

Mix first 4 ingredients together thoroughly; work in flour with hands. Chill dough. Pull off small pieces of chilled dough and work with hands until pliable but not sticky. Roll between palms into pencil-thick strips and shape into small crescents on ungreased cookie sheets. Bake at 350° until set but not brown (about 12 minutes). Remove from cookie sheets when cooled and roll in confectioners sugar. 75 cookies.

SWEDISH SPRITZ

1 cup butter
1 cup sugar
1 well-beaten egg
1/4 teaspoon salt
2 teaspoons vanilla
2-1/2 cups flour

Thoroughly cream butter and sugar; add egg, salt, and vanilla. Beat well. Add sifted flour; mix to smooth dough. Force through cookie press, forming various shapes. Or roll, cut out, and emboss. Bake on ungreased cookie sheet, 2 inches apart, in 350° oven until light brown—about 5 to 8 minutes.

If desired, dip ends of each cookie in chocolate frosting.

BITTERSWEET FROSTING

Melt 1-1/2 squares unsweetened chocolate; cool. Boil 3 tablespoons sugar and 2 tablespoons water until sugar is dissolved. Cool. Stir into chocolate. Let stand until thickened.